The "Putting on the Brakes" ACTIVITY BOOK For Young People with ADHD

♦ ♦ ♦

PATRICIA O. QUINN, M.D.
and
JUDITH M. STERN, M.A.

Illustrations by
NEIL RUSSELL

Magination Press · Washington, DC

Also by the same authors:
PUTTING ON THE BRAKES
Young People's Guide to Understanding
Attention Deficit Hyperactivity Disorder (ADHD)

ISBN: 0-945354-57-6

Copyright © 1993 by Patricia O. Quinn and Judith M. Stern
Illustrations copyright © 1993 by Neil Russell

Figures on page 40 reprinted with permission from *Can You Believe Your Eyes?*
by J. Richard Block and Harold Yuker. New York: Brunner/Mazel, 1989.

Published by
MAGINATION PRESS
An Educational Publishing Foundation Book
American Psychological Association
750 First Street, NE
Washington, DC 20002
1-800-374-2721

Manufactured in the United States of America

Introduction for Parents and Professionals

This **Activity Book** is meant to serve as a companion to our book, *Putting on the Brakes: Young People's Guide to Understanding Attention Deficit Hyperactivity Disorder (ADHD)*. In this book, characteristics of attention deficit hyperactivity disorder were described and young people were offered specific techniques for gaining control. The overwhelming, positive response to our book gave a clear message: Young people welcome the chance to get to know themselves better when the format is respectful, clear and relevant. The adults in their lives are also grateful for a tool that facilitates communication and encourages children's attempts to take responsibility for their own behavior and growth.

Once children have begun to understand what it means to have an attention deficit and take steps to positively influence their own lives, they benefit from the opportunity to try ideas on their own and thus develop a repertoire of behaviors that work for them at home and school. This **Activity Book** introduces a wide range of approaches that can be used to gain mastery over some of the more difficult aspects of ADHD: distractibility, impulsivity, poor planning skills, lack of organization, and a sense of isolation from peers. As children learn to deal with each of these problems in a positive way, their control over their lives is increased.

Along with the message that an attention deficit disorder brings its unique set of problems, comes the clear statement that there are abundant solutions to be tried. In the **Activity Book** they will be shown some new strategies and encouraged to develop even more on their own. Young people learn by doing and by evaluating their successes and mistakes. Working in this **Activity Book** will enable a child to practice many of the concepts previously presented in *Putting on the Brakes* in a way that is fun and developmentally appropriate.

The structure of this **Activity Book** allows it to be used in a variety of ways. While many of the pages can be done independently, others lend themselves to collaborative work with an adult who is significantly involved in the young person's life: a parent, grandparent, counselor, or teacher. Working together with an adult provides an opportunity for discussion of various issues: why a strategy worked or did not, how an adult finds a similar activity relevant in her or his life, or how problems affect one's self-image.

Most pages can be done in any order. Children should not be expected to do many activities at one time. The goal is to make trying new approaches a pleasant venture. Some of the pages are specifically identified as ones to be copied so they can be used repeatedly. Other pages present the activity once but could easily be expanded upon by a teacher, parent or counselor.

There are several places in the **Activity Book** where it is suggested children might be offered reinforcement for meeting specific goals, especially when they have accomplished goals that are particularly difficult in their lives. Adults can choose to manage this reinforcement in a variety of ways. Some children feel rewarded by a the gift of an object they enjoy, while others experience reward from an enthusiastic compliment, a hug, or an extra fifteen minutes delay in bedtime in order to play a game with a parent. We recommend that adults explore with the children ahead of time what type of reinforcement they would like.

We have attempted to address the issues that children, their parents, and teachers have repeatedly identified as particularly problematic in dealing with ADHD. Approaching this topic from our combined backgrounds in medicine and education has enabled us to make recommendations and present activities that address many of the needs of these complex and interesting children.

Patricia O. Quinn, M.D.

Judith M. Stern, M.A.

TABLE OF CONTENTS

INTRODUCTION FOR YOUNG PEOPLE

To all of the boys and girls who use this book:

This **Activity Book** is for young people with Attention Deficit Hyperactivity Disorder (ADHD). It is filled with ideas and suggestions that will help you. It contains information on ADHD, medication, and improving self-control. You will also find pages that deal with homework, planning, keeping organized, and following directions. All of these activities are designed to be fun and to help you understand yourself better and improve specific skills.

This book will be more enjoyable if you complete just a few pages at a time. While working in this book, you may come across a word that you do not understand. There is a glossary on pages 85 and 86 where you can look the word up yourself. If you find you are having difficulty with an activity, be sure to ask for help. There are always people to help you when you need it. These include parents, teachers, tutors, therapists, and counselors.

It is not easy having ADHD. It takes a lot of hard work and practice to become successful. Both of us have worked with many young people with ADHD who have used similar techniques and ideas to solve problems and manage their ADHD. We always enjoy hearing from them regarding our suggestions. If *you* have new ideas, strategies that have worked for you, or questions, please write to us. We would love to hear from you.

Patricia Quinn and Judith Stern
℅ Magination Press
750 First Street, NE
Washington, DC 20002

Part 1

♦♦♦

ALL ABOUT ADHD

ATTENTION   DEFICIT

HYPERACTIVITY   DISORDER

WHAT IS ADHD?

ADHD is a disorder that affects 5 to 10% of all children. That means that in school you may find 1 or 2 children in each class who have a problem with attention. As many as 2,000,000 kids in the United States may have ADHD. It affects boys and girls and can be found in children and adults.

People with attention deficit may have difficulty with focusing, listening, and remembering. They can be **distractible, inattentive, impulsive,** and **hyperactive** (see below). Some have trouble with learning, keeping track of things, finishing what they start, or making and keeping friends.

Not all kids with ADHD have problems in all of these areas. The checklist on the next page will help you take a look at these symptoms and decide which ones describe you.

distractible: you have trouble focusing on just one thing

hyperactive: you have trouble keeping still

impulsive: you often act without thinking

inattentive: you have trouble paying attention

ADHD CHECKLIST

It is important to know how ADHD affects you. Once you have identified what you find difficult about ADHD, you will be better able to come up with plans to overcome these difficulties.

Put a check next to any of the following sentences that describe you or your behavior.

☐ It is hard for me to pay attention to my teacher when he/she is talking.

☐ When I should be working, I am often thinking of other things.

☐ I have trouble starting my work.

☐ I have trouble finishing my work.

☐ I do things without thinking first.

☐ I am disorganized.

☐ I have trouble sitting still.

☐ I have trouble making or keeping friends.

☐ I have trouble following rules.

☐ I forget what I am supposed to do.

☐ It is hard for me to get ready for school on time in the morning.

☐ Noises or other children in the classroom distract me.

☐ I frequently lose things.

Once you have finished this page, show it to your parent, teacher, or counselor. Together, you can talk about ideas to work on some of these areas. You will also find suggestions in this **Activity Book** that may help.

QUESTION:
What part of the body controls attention?

ANSWER: The Brain

Scientists believe that ADHD is caused by problems with the neurotransmitters that send messages from one cell in the brain to another. The parts of the brain that help you slow down and pay attention are not working as well as they should. ADHD does not affect the parts of the brain that involve intelligence. ADHD kids are just as smart or smarter than other kids.

Color and label the picture of the brain below. Use the model on the left to help you.

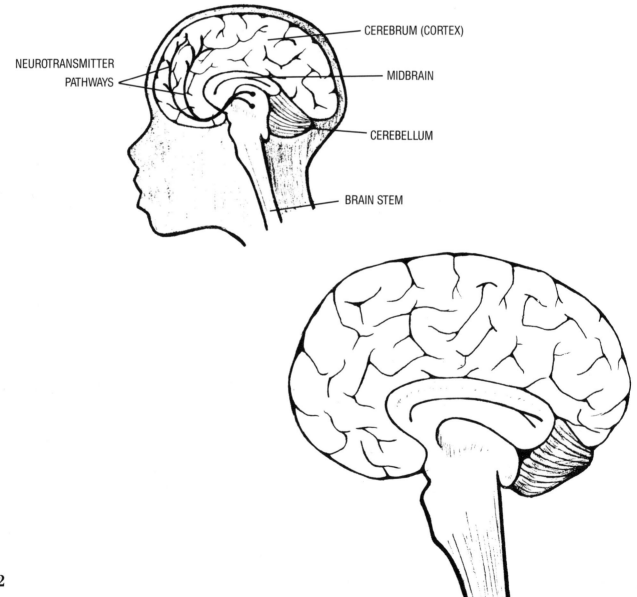

NEUROTRANSMITTER
PATHWAYS

CEREBRUM (CORTEX)

MIDBRAIN

CEREBELLUM

BRAIN STEM

TAKING YOUR MEDICINE

Many kids take medication as part of the treatment for their ADHD. It helps them pay attention and calm down. If you are one of these kids, use this page together with your parents to help you keep track of when you take your medicine. You can also use it to write down any side effects you want to discuss with your doctor. Most kids have no side effects from their medication. If you have questions or concerns about your medicine, be sure to talk with your doctor. He or she can adjust the dose or change your medicine to better help you.

On the form below make a check each time you take a dose of medicine as prescribed by the doctor. Copy this page so you can use it each week.

◆ ◆ ◆

Name: _____

Week of: _____ Weight: _____

Medication name: _____

Dose: _____

Time to be taken: a.m. _____   p.m. _____   p.m. _____

	a.m.	p.m.	p.m.
Monday	_____	_____	_____
Tuesday	_____	_____	_____
Wednesday	_____	_____	_____
Thursday	_____	_____	_____
Friday	_____	_____	_____
Saturday	_____	_____	_____
Sunday	_____	_____	_____

During the week, did you have problems with any of the following:

attention span _____   control of behavior _____   headaches _____

distractibility _____   sitting still _____   stomachaches _____

completing assignments _____   trouble sleeping _____   loss of appetite _____

Questions for the Doctor: _____

_____

_____

HEALTHY SNACKS

When some kids take medicine for their ADHD, they may feel less hungry. This is very common, but it is still important to eat something good for breakfast and lunch. Here are some ideas for healthy snacks. Circle the ones you might like to eat when you are hungry.

a bowl of soup

a bowl of spaghetti

a bowl of rice

crackers and tuna

cinnamon toast

peanut butter and banana sandwich

frozen grapes or blueberries

peanuts and raisins mixed together

a piece of cold chicken

baked potato

celery with peanut butter

grated cheese in a tortilla or pita

a salad

a bowl of chili

crackers and cheese

bagel and cream cheese

a cheese sandwich

sliced fresh fruit

cubes of cheese

yogurt

carrots and celery sticks

applesauce

popcorn

a big slice of watermelon

Don't forget about dinner. It is also important to eat healthy foods then, too. Sometimes if you schedule dinner a little later, you will find yourself hungry enough to eat the full meal.

MY HEALTHY FOOD LIST

Write down the foods that you like and **will** eat. Discuss this list with your parents. You might want to put a list like this in the kitchen or hang it on the refrigerator so that you can read it when you are looking for something to eat. Be sure to include a variety of foods.

◆ MY HEALTHY FOOD LIST ◆

by _____

Foods I like for Breakfast:

_____ _____

_____ _____

Foods I like for Lunch:

_____ _____

_____ _____

Foods I like for Dinner:

_____ _____

_____ _____

Foods I like for Snacks:

_____ _____

_____ _____

_____ _____

HOW DO YOU RELAX?

Many kids with ADHD have difficulty sitting still or being in control. Frequently people will tell them to "calm down!!!" Here are some ways that other kids have found to calm down and relax.

Check the ones that help YOU. List others you have found that also work. If you have never tried to relax, you will find these suggestions worth trying.

☐ Breathe deeply and count to 10.

☐ Listen to music in a quiet place.

☐ Exercise, jog or run.

☐ Take a long bath.

_____

_____

_____

_____

_____

HOW TO CHEER YOURSELF UP

Being able to laugh and have fun is also an important way to calm down and relax. Keeping your sense of humor is very important. Use this page to record...

♦ WISE AND FUNNY SAYINGS FROM FRIENDS AND FAMILY ♦

Funny things my parents say: _____

_____

_____

_____

Funny things my brother/sister says: _____

_____

_____

_____

Funny things my friends say: _____

_____

_____

_____

A word that always makes me laugh: _____

My favorite joke: _____

_____

_____

_____

Be sure to save this page and take a look at it when you are feeling sad or just need a laugh.

MORE JOKES

Here is another page to collect more jokes and funny sayings. When you hear a joke you like, write it here so you won't forget.

SOLVING PROBLEMS

Kids with ADHD sometimes need extra help in solving problems. In order to be a good problem solver, you need to take time to think about choices and pick the best solution. Practice helps, and so does talking over problems with an adult who can offer additional suggestions. This page will give you practice in finding solutions to problems.

Read each of the problems below. Check the solution or solutions you think best for each one. You might want to make up some of your own solutions as well. Put them on the blank lines after each story.

◆ Sandy was sitting in her classroom before class had started. Her good friend walked into the room with a new haircut that Sandy did not like. Sandy should:

☐ immediately call out that her friend has an ugly haircut.

☐ not make any comments until her friend has asked her.

☐ keep her opinion to herself.

☐ other ideas _____

_____

_____

_____

◆ Joe has a hard time paying attention to his science teacher. Which of these actions might be helpful while his teacher is talking?

☐ Avoid sitting next to his friend.

☐ Read a science book.

☐ Try hard to look at the teacher each time she speaks.

☐ Try taking notes on important things that the teacher says.

☐ Close his eyes while listening.

☐ Other ideas_____

_____

_____

_____

♦ Your cousin has a reputation for losing things all the time. Which of these suggestions would you make to her?

☐ Set up her room with specific places to put things.

☐ Carry important items around with her all of the time.

☐ Clean her backpack out at least once a week.

☐ Keep a box at the front door for school materials.

☐ Other ideas _____

_____

_____

_____

♦ At recess you find you usually have no one to play with. You could:

☐ bring a ball from home to start a game.

☐ pick a fight.

☐ brag about your new computer.

☐ start a conversation with one or two other kids you like.

☐ other ideas _____

_____

_____

_____

♦ Lee is always in trouble because he has a quick temper. He could:

☐ try counting to 10 and taking a deep breath when something annoys him.

☐ ask for a punching bag to keep in his room.

☐ cry and scream in front of others.

☐ other ideas _____

_____

_____

_____

LEARNING FROM MISTAKES

Everyone makes mistakes. The trick is to learn not to make the same one again.

Write a story about something that happened to you that caused a problem or got you into trouble.

_____

_____

_____

_____

_____

_____

_____

Write the solution you used here. _____

_____

_____

_____

Why didn't it work? _____

_____

_____

What would you do differently next time? _____

_____

_____

_____

> **Everybody makes mistakes. We can all learn from our mistakes.**

WHAT DO YOU KNOW ABOUT ADHD?

Now that you know more about ADHD, see how many of these questions you can answer. Complete the sentences below by <u>underlining</u> the correct answer from the words in parenthesis.

1. ADHD stands for (attention, detention) deficit hyperactivity disorder.

2. Kids with ADHD are (smart, dumb).

3. (Exercising, Getting angrier) can help you calm down and relax.

4. ADHD may be caused by (too few neurotransmitters, too much energy) in the brain.

5. Impulsivity is acting (before, after) thinking.

6. Some kids with ADHD are helped by taking (soda, medicine) to help them pay attention.

7. Only a (doctor, teacher) can prescribe medicine for ADHD.

8. Kids with ADHD have feelings. They (should, should not) talk about these feelings with others.

9. (Potato chips, An apple) makes a healthy snack.

10. (Only a few, Lots of) kids have ADHD.

11. If you are hyperactive you may have difficulty (sitting still, thinking).

12. It's (okay, not okay) to make mistakes.

13. Kids with ADHD (can, cannot) be successful in life.

Answers on page 83

Part 2
♦♦♦
ALL ABOUT YOU

Here is the good news about having ADHD. All kids with ADHD have good qualities they can be proud of. They can be:

WESOME

ETERMINED

APPY

AZZLING

This section of the book will help you get to know yourself and better appreciate your many good qualities. It will also show you some ways to get support and to be a better friend.

WHAT ARE YOU LIKE?

Which of the following sentences describe YOU?

Put a check next to the ones that do. Add your own words in the blanks at the end.

☐ I am full of energy.

☐ I have many good ideas.

☐ I am good at sports.

☐ I have a good sense of humor.

☐ I am creative.

☐ I like people.

☐ I like to talk.

☐ I am a good reader.

☐ I am good at art.

☐ I am good at math.

☐ I am helpful to others.

☐ I am strong.

☐ I am smart.

☐ I am _____

_____

_____

_____

> **Always remember your good qualities.**
> **They are a very important part of who you are.**
> **People appreciate these parts of you.**

HOW DO YOU FEEL?

Kids with ADHD have all kinds of feelings. Circle the feelings that you have sometimes. At the bottom of the page, there is room for you to add other feelings you have had.

Energetic	Confused
Athletic	Overloaded
Creative	Angry
Sensitive	Frustrated
Attractive	Misunderstood
Smart	Picked on
Friendly	Forgetful
Caring	Unpopular
Curious	Impatient
Special	Scared
Artistic	Dumb
Humorous	Teased
Imaginative	Anxious
Enthusiastic	Disorganized
Adaptable	Tense
Happy	Hyper
_____	_____
_____	_____
_____	_____
_____	_____

Share this page with your parents or counselor.

WHAT MAKES YOU HAVE GOOD FEELINGS?

Draw a picture or make a list of things that make you feel good.

YOU ARE A WONDERFUL PERSON!!!

Ask your parents, a friend, and a teacher to write down something they think is great about YOU. When this page is completed, copy it and hang it over your desk or bed, so you can look at it often.

parent's compliment: _____

_____

_____

_____

teacher's compliment: _____

_____

_____

_____

friend's compliment: _____

_____

_____

_____

give yourself a compliment here: _____

_____

_____

_____

A STORY FOR YOU

An Apple, A Pear, A Plum, A Cherry
by Rusty Clauss

Once there was a boy who lived in Alltime. When he was five years old, he went to school. In the summer he played with his friends. He liked the summer. He liked his friends. He liked school.

But, by the time he was seven, he did not like school. By the time he was eight, he did not like some of his friends. And by the time he was nine, he did not even like summer.

One green and gold day, he went for a walk. By and by he came to a woods and went into it. There he sat down in the dark and looked out at the sunshine.

One day while the boy sat in the woods, an old man walked by. "Boy," said the old man, "why are you sitting in the dark?"

"Because I am not happy, Old One," said the boy.

"I see," said the old man. And he sat down with the boy. "Why is it that you are not happy?" asked the old man.

"I am not happy because I am stupid," said the boy.

"And how do you know that you are stupid?" asked the old man.

The boy looked out at the sunshine and said, "I know it because my little sister can read books that I cannot read. My friends can solve problems that I cannot solve. My teacher gives me papers that I cannot finish. That is how I know."

"I see," said the old man. "And was your life always this way?"

The boy thought back over his life. And he said, "No, when I was six, I was happy most of the time. When I was seven I was happy some of the time. When I was eight, I was happy a little of the time."

"Now you are nine," said the old man, "and are you not happy at all?"

"No, I am not," said the boy. "My friends laugh at me. They call me names. I get mad and I hit them because they are right."

The old man got up and said, "Come. Walk with me." And he gave the boy his

hand and they walked away from the woods. The path led them to a farm. Here the old man stopped and said, "What trees do you see here?"

The boy looked at the trees and said quickly, "I see cherry trees and plum trees. I see apple trees and pear trees."

"And which tree is the best?" asked the old man.

The boy said, "I like. . ."

"No," said the old man. "I did not ask which tree you LIKE the best. I asked which tree IS the best."

And the boy thought about the trees. "There is not one that is best," he said at last.

The old man stopped smiling. "But the cherry and the plum come first. The apple and the pear come late in the year. Are not the cherry and the plum best?"

Then the boy saw that this was a test and he was afraid. But he answered, "No, Old One. They all are pretty in the spring. They all give us shade in the summer. And they all give us good things to eat."

Then the old man's face became dark. "But the apple tree takes longer! Is this not bad?"

"No, Old One," the boy said in a small voice. "It is the way of apple trees."

"Then apple trees are bad!!" The old man's voice was like thunder.

But the boy said, "No. It is just that it is an apple tree. Apple trees are good!"

Then the old man smiled. "You have learned something," he said.

"What?" asked the boy.

"That I will not tell you," said the old man. "That is for you to find out." And he walked on.

But the boy stayed and looked at the trees. And at last he smiled.

Rusty Clauss, a teacher for 21 years, is now a theatre consultant, writer and director.

ME AND MY ADHD

Complete these sentences. When you are finished, you might want to share them with an adult or a group of other ADHD kids. The people you share this page with will learn many important things about you.

♦ Paying Attention

I have difficulty paying attention when _____

I concentrate best when _____

The best place for me to sit in the classroom is _____

When I am not paying attention, I like my teacher to _____

_____

♦ What I Don't Like to Hear

I don't like it when my mother or father tells me _____

_____

I don't like it when my teacher says _____

_____

♦ What I Find Helpful

Some things that help when I feel like I need to move around are _____

_____

Time out works well for me when _____

I like to talk to _____ because they understand me.

Some things that make me want to try harder are _____

_____

_____

MORE ABOUT ME

Your ADHD is only one part of you. There are *many* things about you that make you SPECIAL. Here is a chance to "talk" about yourself.

Fill in these sentences so they describe you.

I am very good at _____.

This year I have gotten better at _____.

My favorite subject at school is _____.

The subject I like least is _____.

One of the best books I ever read was _____.

If I could travel anywhere, I would like to go to _____.

When I play with a friend, I like to _____.

I like to _____ with my family.

My favorite meal is _____, _____ and _____.

If I could plan the perfect day, this is what I would want to do in the

    morning _____

    afternoon _____

    evening _____

Something about myself that I would like to change is _____

_____

_____.

What I like best about myself is _____

_____

_____.

This page can also be shared with someone who is important to you.

FINDING HELP

There are many ways that a child with ADHD can get support. See if you can find these words in the puzzle below:

SUPPORT   HELP   PRAISE   ENCOURAGEMENT
          STRUCTURE   REWARDS   FRIENDS   LOVE

E	C	D	P	X	S	Y	T	V	W	H	E	L	F	E	R	I	J	Z	L
I	N	N	L	E	W	Z	Y	S	E	F	W	R	A	N	A	D	B	G	C
H	M	C	R	A	P	U	O	G	E	R	J	L	A	K	P	J	X	G	V
C	A	I	O	J	S	K	B	D	K	I	C	G	R	O	T	A	S	B	N
M	B	L	B	U	P	C	D	M	P	E	G	J	C	B	I	J	U	A	Y
Z	C	D	O	W	R	P	N	T	M	N	Z	Y	N	M	L	E	P	F	K
H	G	J	Y	F	F	A	B	C	G	D	E	H	S	R	W	X	P	G	S
M	R	N	A	E	G	T	G	W	Z	S	Y	T	R	A	G	W	O	P	S
L	E	M	G	L	C	L	W	E	Z	G	H	J	K	F	E	U	R	T	G
O	W	F	G	O	N	B	R	P	M	E	G	X	G	T	M	N	T	P	Q
Z	A	G	P	A	X	T	H	A	N	E	C	G	W	Q	O	R	X	Z	W
S	R	U	C	P	O	R	E	H	E	L	N	A	D	H	D	F	R	E	N
G	D	E	R	E	N	D	E	N	C	O	R	T	H	E	P	R	G	F	D
X	S	T	R	U	C	T	U	R	E	A	R	W	G	A	L	X	Y	W	V
K	A	I	P	A	X	T	H	A	N	X	C	G	W	Q	O	R	X	Z	W
Q	W	E	R	T	Y	A	S	D	F	G	H	J	K	L	V	B	P	N	V
E	S	T	Y	U	L	G	I	T	C	Q	N	L	E	J	E	Q	J	L	Q
N	B	A	I	N	C	G	H	E	L	P	W	J	I	Q	P	O	G	X	Y
A	D	F	H	G	T	Z	A	W	V	G	J	P	R	A	I	S	E	G	E

**Sometimes Help Seems Hard to Find, But It Is There All Around You.
You Are Not Alone!!!**

Answers on page 83

CALLING FOR HELP

The telephone can be a very helpful way to reach someone when you have a question or need some assistance. Fill out this phone list and hang it up in a place where you can always find it.

NAME   TELEPHONE NUMBER

Emergency _____   _____

Parents' work numbers

    Mom _____   _____

    Dad _____   _____

Helpful neighbor _____   _____

Relative you like to talk to _____   _____

Homework buddy _____   _____

Friend _____   _____

Doctor _____   _____

MAKING FRIENDS

Making friends is not always easy for someone with ADHD, but with practice you can make it come out right. What you choose to do together with your friend can be important!

Write down 5 things you really like to do. Think of someone you would like to do each of these with.

Here is an example:

I like

BOWLING

This might be fun to do with

JEREMY

Now you try it:

I like   This might be fun to do with

1. _____   _____

2. _____   _____

3. _____   _____

4. _____   _____

5. _____   _____

Talk with your parents about helping you set up a special time with someone you like.

FRIENDSHIP

◆ TIME SPENT WITH A FRIEND IS SPECIAL ◆

TAKING TURNS

To be a good friend, you need to be able to take turns when you play games.

On these pages you will find some suggestions for games that will help you practice taking turns while you have fun playing with one other person. When you get good at it, try playing with two or more other kids.

♦ **Games to Play with One Other Person**

Cards

Catch with a ball

Chess

Checkers

Hangman

Hopscotch

♦ **Games to Play with Two or More**

Jump rope

Board games

Card games

Charades

Make up a play or put on a show

add your own favorite games here

_____

_____

_____

_____

Think of a time that you really had fun with a friend. Write four rules to follow that really made it work. The first one is done for you.

1. Discuss and decide on the rules <u>before</u> you begin the game.

2. _____

3. _____

4. _____

Try following these rules the next time you play with a friend.

Give yourself a grade on how well you did at following your own rules.

Name of Game	Outstanding	Good	Could Be Better
_____	_____	_____	_____
_____	_____	_____	_____
_____	_____	_____	_____
_____	_____	_____	_____

GETTING ORGANIZED

Keeping organized can help make life easier. Try to create specific places to keep your belongings and school materials. Then you will be able to find them when you need them.

HELP! Jimmy is in trouble.
He needs to clean his room before his mother gets home.

Draw a line from each item to a place where it can be put away.

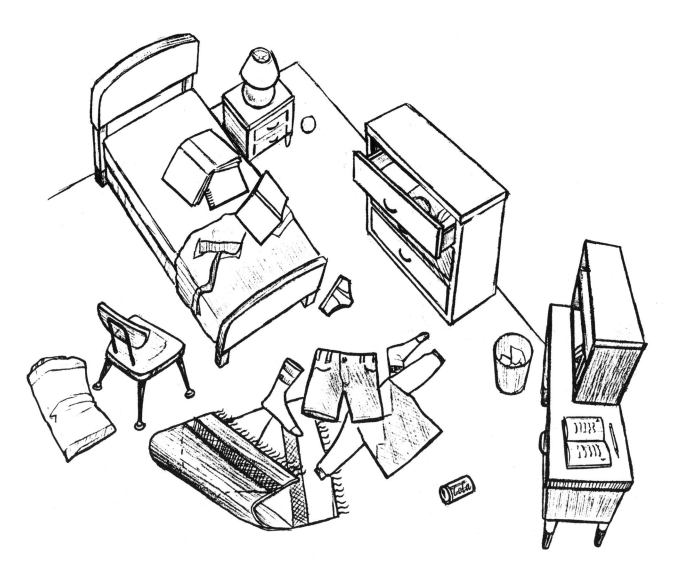

To see how Jimmy's room looks after you have helped him, turn to Answers, page 83.

Part 3

♦ ♦ ♦

SHARPENING YOUR SKILLS

In sports to be a good athlete, you need to practice. Practice is important to improve other skills as well. Kids with ADHD sometimes have difficulty paying attention to details, following directions, finishing an assignment, organizing, sequencing, or managing time. This next section will help you practice and sharpen these skills.

WHAT DO YOU SEE?

When you look at a picture, what do you see? At first you see one thing. Now look again. Can you see something else?

A. What is this? Look again.

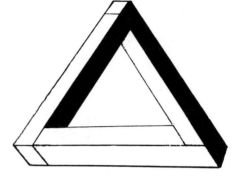

B. Are the black sides inside or outside?

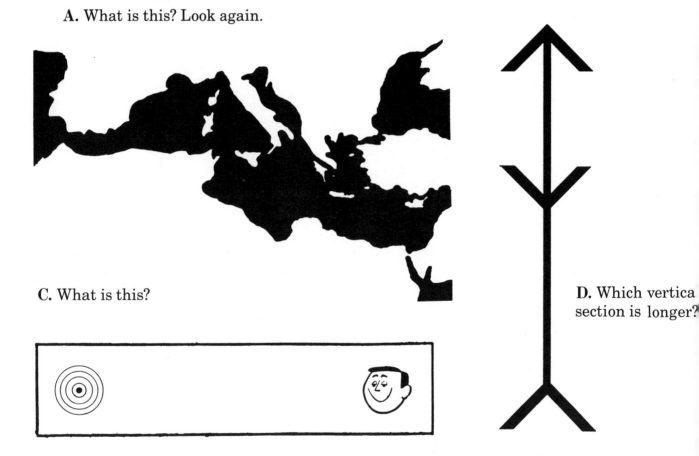

C. What is this?

D. Which vertical section is longer?

E. Can you make the face disappear?

Answers on page 84

WHAT IS WRONG HERE?

Paying attention to details is also important. It helps you find mistakes and is an essential skill for being a good reader and writer. It can be fun and makes you a good observer.

What can you find wrong with this picture?

LOOK CAREFULLY!

To be a good reader, it is important to look at words CAREFULLY, so that you don't mistake them for other words that look very similar. Be sure to look at the beginning, middle, and ending of all words.

Here is an activity to give you some practice looking at words.

Circle the two words in each row that are the SAME. If this seems easy to you, try doing it *quickly* and accurately. It is good practice.

1.	slip	slop	slip	slap
2.	quit	quite	quilt	quit
3.	since	sense	since	science
4.	happier	happiness	happiest	happiest
5.	shingle	single	single	singer
6.	coordinated	coordinator	coordinate	coordinated
7.	were	where	we're	were
8.	choose	chose	cheese	chose
9.	where	there	there	their
10.	hoping	helping	hopping	hopping
11.	flight	fight	fright	flight
12.	heartless	heartfelt	heartfelt	heartburn
13.	hematoid	hematosis	hematozoa	hematosis

WHAT'S THE RIGHT ORDER?

Doing things in the right order (sequence) can also be very important. Can you imagine...

Putting your boots on after you have gone out in the snow?
Washing your face before you get out of bed?

Put the following events in the right order. Put a 1 in front of the event that happens first, a 2 in front of the next step, and so on.

A   _____   Jeff broke a window.

       _____   Jeff hit the ball in his yard.

       _____   Jeff picked up the bat.

B   _____   Next, I bought a new pencil.

       _____   First, I bought two candy bars.

       _____   Finally, I bought the tape I wanted.

       _____   Now, I have no money.

C   _____   Ted cooked dinner.

       _____   Jed put the dishes away.

       _____   Ned dried the dishes.

       _____   Ed washed the dishes.

Answers on page 84

TELLING THE STORY

Can you arrange these pictures in the correct order to tell what happened in the story? Fill in a number in the empty box at the corner of each picture to tell what happens first, second, third, and fourth.

Answers on page 84

FINISH WHAT YOU START

An important part of being a successful student is finishing your work. The finished product is what you will be judged on. So for each job you do, start at the beginning and keep at it until you are finished. You will be proud of your completed work.

See if you can stick with the dot-to-dot activity below until it is finished.

Remember: Don't give up! Keep at it.

TRY IT!

Sometimes a task can feel very complicated, or look difficult at first. But when you actually try, you find you can succeed.

Try working on this maze slowly and carefully.

Don't be afraid to ask for help if you need it.

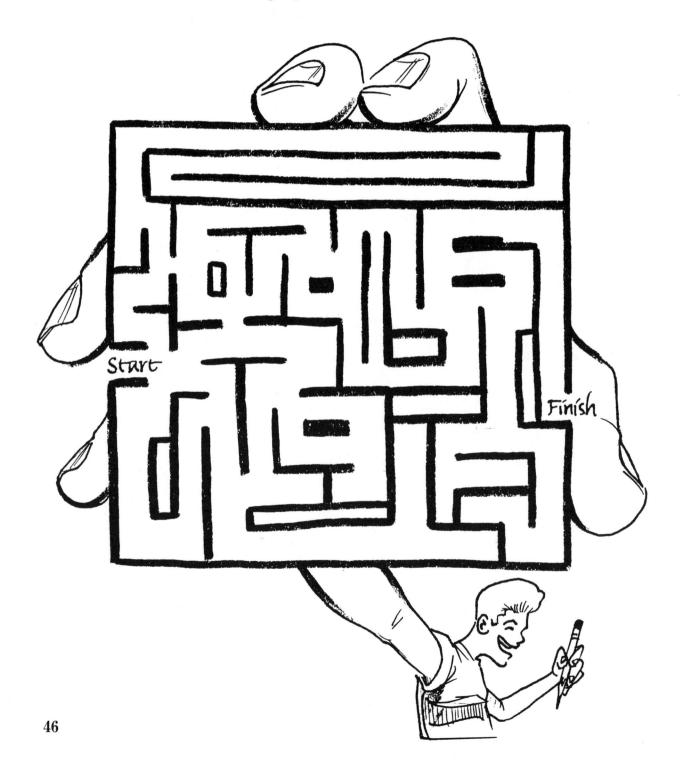

DIRECTION INSPECTION

Now let's practice following directions! Be a Direction Inspector.

When you read directions, it is very important to pay attention to the **little** words that tell you how to mark your answers. Examples of "direction words" are: match, circle, connect, cross out, and underline. Many kids find it useful to highlight the special words in directions that explain how to do an assignment. You can highlight by circling, underlining, or using a highlighter marker.

In the directions below, <u>underline</u> the words or words in each sentence that you think are the most important for telling you how to do the exercise.

Example: <u>Circle</u> the best answer.

1. Underline the correct definition.

2. Write all your answers in cursive.

3. On this test, you need to match the answer on the left with the synonym in the right column. Draw a line to each correct answer.

4. Find the mistake in each paragraph and cross it out.

5. Copy the answer to each math problem into the answer column on the right side of the page.

6. Fill in the circle next to each correct answer.

7. Check the first five examples on each page. Show your work.

8. Select and answer two of the following five questions.

DRAWING REMINDERS

Many kids with attention problems find it helpful to draw reminders when someone gives them oral directions. That way there is something to look back at later if they have forgotten what to do. Here is some practice in recording directions.

♦ Your parent tells you to remember to do three things after school: feed the dog, put out the trash, and hang up your coat.

Draw three easy pictures that would remind you of what you need to do when you get home.

♦ Today after school, instead of going straight home, you have a doctor's appointment and baseball practice. Then you are going to your grandmother's house for dinner.

Draw pictures to remind yourself where to go.

WRITING REMINDERS

Writing brief notes is another way to help remember what you have to do.

Your teacher gives you the following directions. Write a short list to remind yourself what to do. Write only a few words and <u>not</u> full sentences.

> "For school tomorrow remember to bring: permission slip for the class trip to the museum and money for the trip, your gym shoes and shorts for third period, and your math test, which must be signed at the top by one of your parents."

Write your reminder notes here:

_____

_____

_____

_____

_____

Now try this:

> "Don't forget that your biography book report is due tomorrow. It must be in a folder with a cover and a bibliography. Make sure that the title, your name, and the date are written neatly on the cover. When you bring it in, you must put it in the red tray on my desk by 9 o'clock."

Write your notes here:

_____

_____

_____

_____

_____

MAKING LISTS

Lists can be helpful for remembering important things. Try this activity.

Make a list of ten things you want to remember to bring the next time you go on a vacation.

1. _____   6. _____

2. _____   7. _____

3. _____   8. _____

4. _____   9. _____

5. _____   10. _____

Pretend you are leaving on that vacation tomorrow. Your friend has agreed to take care of your pet. Write down 5 things that she needs to do each day.

1. _____

2. _____

3. _____

4. _____

5. _____

FOLLOWING A RECIPE

You have been practicing following directions and doing things in the right order. This is because directions are a part of everyday life. For example, when you cook it is important to follow the recipe exactly. You must first read the directions carefully. Prepare your ingredients ahead of time, and do all steps in the correct order. This will help you make the food come out right.

Try this recipe for French Toast. Ask an adult to help.

FRENCH TOAST

Ingredients:

2 slices of bread	cinnamon
1 egg	2 tablespoons of margarine
1/4 cup milk	syrup, jelly or applesauce

You will need:

1 fork	1 pancake turner
1 wide bowl	1 medium frying pan

Directions:

Break the egg into a bowl. Beat the egg with a fork. Pour the milk in with the egg. Beat them together. Sprinkle in a small amount of cinnamon. Melt margarine in frying pan, using low heat. Dip one slice of bread into the egg-milk mixture. Gently turn the bread over to cover the other side. Do the same with the other slice of bread. Put both slices into the frying pan. Turn each slice over when the bottom is golden brown. When the second side of each slice is brown, turn off the stove and put the French Toast on a plate. Spread with syrup, jelly or applesauce.

Part 4

◆◆◆

SUCCEEDING
IN SCHOOL

ADHD kids are smart, but they still might find school to be somewhat difficult. Intelligence is important, but so is being organized, managing projects well, and checking over work. Sometimes, this is where kids with attention problems need some extra help. In this section, you will find many ideas to try so that you succeed in school.

PROOFREADING YOUR WORK

School assignments need to be done accurately. The skills you have developed for finding mistakes and looking carefully will help when correcting your own work. This skill is called "proofreading."

How many mistakes can you find on this page of math problems?

See if you can do a better job of checking than the person who handed in this paper.

1. $7 \times 9 = 63$

2. $4 + 7 = 11$

3. $21 + 46 = 66$

4. $8 \times 6 = 46$

5. $3 + 21 = 63$

6. $6 \times 12 = 64$

7. $9 - 4 = 5$

8. $33 + 22 = 66$

9.
$$\begin{array}{r} 836 \\ -\ 567 \\ \hline 1403 \end{array}$$

10.
$$\begin{array}{r} 560 \\ \times\ 21 \\ \hline 11{,}760 \end{array}$$

11. $279 \div 3 = 93$

12.
$$\begin{array}{r} 2\ 1/2 \\ +\ 7\ 1/4 \\ \hline 9\ 2/4 \end{array}$$

Remember: Everyone makes mistakes, but only people who check can find them.

Correct answers on page 84

CORRECTING YOUR WORK

Jerry's teacher has a headache. After checking so many papers, he needs a break. Look over this assignment that Jerry did.

Use a red pen to correct any mistakes he made in punctuation, capitalization, or spelling.

Hint: After you are done, walk away for a few minutes. Then come back and look at the page again. Can you find any more mistakes?

Last weak we went to visit my ant & uncle, who live in detroit michigan When ant Jane saw me, she said in a lowd voice, Youve really growne since last year! We had fun being together Next year, I hop we can spend more then too days in detroit.

Corrected paragraph on page 84

MANAGING YOUR TIME

DON'T RUSH THROUGH YOUR WORK
DO SLOW DOWN AND WORK CAREFULLY

DON'T TRY TO DO A JOB ALL AT ONCE
DO BREAK IT DOWN INTO SMALLER PARTS

DON'T LEAVE EVERYTHING UNTIL THE LAST MINUTE
DO MAKE A SCHEDULE

DON'T TRY TO DO EVERYTHING BY YOURSELF
DO WORK WITH OTHERS. IT'S MORE FUN

TIMING HOMEWORK

Learning to manage time can help you with your homework. Pick one of your homework assignments for today. Take a guess at how long it will take you to complete it.

Assignment name _____.

How long do you think it will take to complete this work?

Write your guess here: _____

Have someone time how long it actually takes you.

Write that time here: _____

How close was your guess? _____

Did the work take more or less time than you thought? _____

Why do you think this happened? _____

_____

_____

Try this again with another assignment on another day.

Assignment name _____

How long do you think it will take? _____

How long did it take? _____

The more you practice estimating the time you need, the better you will get at it.

PLANNING PROJECTS

In addition to your daily homework, larger projects will also be assigned by your teachers. They expect their students to be able to do a little of the work each day. This makes a big assignment more manageable. When you find out that you have a large project assigned to you

DON'T PANIC!   DON'T AVOID THE JOB!   PLAN!!

Make a schedule. Decide to do a part of the project, study for the test, or work on the assignment each day until it is due.

Here is an example of a work plan for a science project:

Monday: Decide on topic for project.

Tuesday: Get books out of the library on your topic.

Wednesday and Thursday: Take notes from the books.

Friday: Draw diagrams and labels.

Saturday and Sunday: Build project.

Monday: Look everything over and make sure you are satisfied.

Tuesday: Project DUE. Hand it in.

MAKING A WORK SCHEDULE

Now try this: Your friend has a big report to do. She has asked you to help her figure out what she should do each day of this week so she will be done in time. Today is Saturday and the report is due next Friday. She has one week to get everything done.

Here is her homework assignment. Next to each day, write what your friend should do.

Read pages 42–60 in the book about the presidents. Write one page about the president *you* found most interesting. Write one page on the president about whom you learned many new things. Make a cover for your report. Be sure you write a rough draft and a final copy.

Work Schedule for your friend

Saturday   _____

Sunday   _____

Monday   _____

Tuesday   _____

Wednesday _____

Thursday   _____

> **Remember: The more you spread things out and do a little at a time, the easier a big job will feel!**

AFTER-SCHOOL SCHEDULE

A daily schedule can help you plan your after-school time so that you still have your own free time.

When you get home from school, work out a schedule for the afternoon and evening that will include: homework assignments, studying for tests, reading, chores, snacks and dinner, and special activities for the day. Don't forget to put in short breaks. You deserve them, and they help you concentrate better.

Use the next page to write down your schedule. Here is a sample to give you some ideas:

3:30 Arrive home

4:00 Spelling homework

4:30 Free time

5:15 Math

5:45 Read for book report

6:00 Dinner

7:00 Practice trumpet

7:20 Finish homework

8:00 Chores

8:15 Free time

9:00 Get ready for bed

9:30 Bed

AFTER-SCHOOL PLAN

♦ Use this page to plan your after-school time.

For _____ (day of the week)

(You might want to review this plan with an adult before you start.)

3:00 _____

3:30 _____

4:00 _____

4:30 _____

5:00 _____

5:30 _____

6:00 _____

6:30 _____

7:00 _____

7:30 _____

8:00 _____

8:30 _____

9:00 _____

9:30 _____

10:00 _____

You may want to make copies of this page so you can make a schedule for each day of the week.

HOW YOU STUDY BEST

Sometimes where, when, and how you study makes a BIG difference in how well you do. Below you will find a list of study suggestions. If you have already tried some of these different ways to study, rate how they work for you. If they are new ideas, give them a try and see if they are helpful. Then come back to this page and rate them.

Study Techniques	doesn't work for me	can be somewhat helpful	works well	This is great!
Studying in the morning	_____	_____	_____	_____
Studying in the afternoon	_____	_____	_____	_____
Studying after dinner	_____	_____	_____	_____
Studying by myself	_____	_____	_____	_____
Studying with a friend	_____	_____	_____	_____
Studying with a tutor or parent	_____	_____	_____	_____
Working in a quiet room	_____	_____	_____	_____
Working in a noisy place	_____	_____	_____	_____
Working with quiet music in the background	_____	_____	_____	_____
Studying while I sit at a desk	_____	_____	_____	_____
Studying while I lie on a bed	_____	_____	_____	_____
Studying while I walk around	_____	_____	_____	_____

	doesn't work for me	can be somewhat helpful	works well	This is great!
Writing important information down over and over	_____	_____	_____	_____
Reading my notes out loud	_____	_____	_____	_____
Having my parents give me practice tests	_____	_____	_____	_____
Listening to my notes on a tape recorder	_____	_____	_____	_____
Working in an area with bright lights	_____	_____	_____	_____
Working in an area lit by a lamp	_____	_____	_____	_____
Studying when I am tired	_____	_____	_____	_____
Studying when I am wide awake	_____	_____	_____	_____
Studying after I have exercised	_____	_____	_____	_____
Studying after a snack or meal	_____	_____	_____	_____

**Remember to use the ideas that work well for you.
It will make things easier and you will see positive results.**

STUDY SUGGESTIONS

Here are some study suggestions that other kids have found helpful. After you have tried them, check the ones you find useful. Add some of your own at the bottom. You can discuss this page with your teacher, parent or tutor.

☐ If you have many facts to memorize, try saying them into a tape recorder. Then listen to them over and over again on the tape.

☐ Make up flash cards (with the answers on the back). Study from them. Try cards for spelling words, vocabulary words, math facts or science questions.

☐ Walk around or pedal a stationary bicycle as you study.

☐ If you have to read a whole chapter, try reading one page at a time. When you finish each page write a sentence or two about the main facts or ideas on that page.

☐ Use different colors to underline important ideas in your notes or books.

☐ Try drawing a diagram or map to help you understand an idea.

☐ Discuss information that will be on the test with someone else (another student in the class, a parent, or a tutor).

☐ Have someone make up a practice test for you to take.

☐ Other ideas: _____

_____

Which three techniques work best for you when studying?

1. _____

2. _____

3. _____

Remember to use them often.

TEACHERS' IDEAS

Teachers have lots of good ideas to help you. Ask your teacher for some of her or his suggestions. Here are some ideas that teachers have shared with us.

Try these or talk them over with your teacher to see if they might work for you.

♦ Keeping Your Homework Organized

Elizabeth Silverberg, a 6th grade teacher in Demarest, New Jersey, suggests using three separate folders:

1. "To Do" folder – Everything in this folder needs to be done for homework that day. Assignment sheets should be in this folder.

2. "In Progress" folder – This folder contains any work that needs to be handed in some time in the future (such as at the end of the week or at the end of the month). Students need to check this folder every day.

3. "Done" folder – This contains everything that students have finished and are ready to hand in.

♦ Remembering Your Homework

Maureen Henrickson, a 3rd grade teacher in Sutton, Massachusetts, suggests using a pocket folder with an 8 × 10 sheet attached to the front. Write the daily homework assignment for each subject on the front cover. Completed homework can be returned to school the next day in the same folder. Your teacher and parents can write any comments they have at the bottom of the front sheet.

♦ Remembering Long-Term Assignments

Penny Newman, a resource teacher in White Plains, New York suggests writing all of your long-term assignments in an assignment book using a red pen. This makes the assignment stand out so you cannot miss it. Rewrite the assignment in red each day until it is due. This serves as a frequent reminder.

Teachers' Ideas *(continued)*

◆ Writing a Story

Deborah Ciment, a 5th grade teacher in Rockville, Maryland suggests that before you write a story or essay, you write down as many nouns, adjectives, and verbs that you can think of that are related to the topic assigned. This list can be used as you are working on your assignment. It will give you many ideas to make your story or essay richer.

◆ Problems with Sitting Still

Kathy Ruddick, a student teacher in Paxton, Massachusetts suggests that if you have a great deal of difficulty staying in your seat for a long period of time, you ask your teacher for a "walk pass" (something like a bathroom pass). The "walk pass" allows you to walk around in the classroom or hall when you just need to move around. You should try to notice when you need to use the pass the most. You should also try to work on decreasing the number of times you use it each day.

◆ Understanding Material

Pam Smith, an educational specialist in Washington, DC suggests that when you have trouble understanding material that you are reading or hearing, you should "Run a movie camera in your head." By that she means to VISUALIZE information. "Running the camera" allows you to put information into a picture in your mind. When you "see" what the information is telling you, it almost immediately becomes more understandable. Sitting with your eyes closed, you should be better able to SEE and UNDERSTAND.

◆ Following Directions

Paula Fiorillo, a 4th grade teacher in Shrewsbury, Massachusetts suggests asking your teacher if you can use a tape recorder with headphones to listen to the directions for all of the assignments to be covered in class each day. The tape should include all the necessary information to complete the work in each subject. You can then listen again privately to the directions as many times as you need. The headphones can also help to filter out some of the distracting noises in the classroom.

♦ Checklists for Keeping Organized

Paula Arons, a reading teacher in Cincinnati, Ohio recommends that her students use the following checklists to stay organized. They keep these lists on the front of their notebooks so that they can use them every day.

Before I leave school I will check to make sure I have:

Every assignment written down in my assignment book.

Every book I need.

All materials I need to do my assignments.

All notes that need to be seen by my parents.

Any and all tests that need to be signed.

All folders and notebooks I need.

My bookbag.

Mon	Tues	Wed	Thurs	Fri

Week of _____

Before I leave home for school I will check to make sure I have:

All of my completed assignments

All of my assignments in the correct folders.

All assignments, folders, and notebooks in my bookbag.

All books I need in my bookbag.

All materials I need for school in my bookbag.

All notes and signed tests in my bookbag.

My bookbag.

Mon	Tues	Wed	Thurs	Fri

Week of _____

You may want to make copies of these checklists to use every day.

TEST PLANNER

The next time you have a test, use this page as your "study helper." Ask an adult to help you the first few times you use it. Try to complete this planner several days before the test.

1. Subject of the test _____

2. Date of the test _____

3. Number of days that you have to study _____

4. What do you need to know for the test? _____

5. How do you plan to study for this test? _____

_____

_____

_____

(Use some ideas from the Study Suggestions, page 64)

6. Develop a work schedule using the form below:

Day	Material to study	Time scheduled
_____	_____	_____
_____	_____	_____
_____	_____	_____
_____	_____	_____
_____	_____	_____
_____	_____	_____

> **Remember: Start your studying several days before the test.**
> **Divide up the work!!!**

TEST CHECK UP

How did you do on your test?

Could do better _____

Good _____

Excellent _____

What type of mistakes did you make on this test?

examples:
- ☐ Didn't study long enough
- ☐ Didn't know vocabulary
- ☐ Didn't know factual information
- ☐ Didn't check my work over
- ☐ Didn't write enough on short essays
- ☐ Didn't finish test
- ☐ Other

_____

_____

_____

What did you do that was most helpful for this test?

_____

_____

_____

What study ideas will you try for the next test?

_____

_____

_____

Talk about ways to avoid mistakes and do better the next time with your teacher or counselor.

REMEMBERING WHAT YOU READ

When you are reading a book or a unit with many chapters, you can remember more of the material by trying some of these ideas. Check the suggestions that work best for you.

☐ Write a sentence or two about each page.

☐ Write a summary (3 sentences) after each chapter.

☐ List the important characters of a story as you come across them.

☐ Write down important dates and places.

☐ List words found in bold print and include their definitions.
  This is good to do on cards with the definitions on the back.

☐ Make a short outline of the facts on each page.

☐ Look at the pictures and read the captions.

☐ Draw a map, diagram, or picture about the information you have read.

☐ Draw a time line to help with dates or the sequence of events.

☐ Record main ideas on a tape recorder as you read.

☐ Write your own study questions after each chapter.

GETTING THE INFORMATION

In school you will often read pages filled with important information. Writing things down helps many people "hold on" to facts better. Read the following paragraph. Then follow the directions below.

On an autumn day in 1991, Governor Bill Clinton stood in front of the Old Statehouse Building in Little Rock, Arkansas to announce his plan to run for president of the United States. At the Democratic National Convention held in New York City in July of 1992, he was chosen to be the Democratic Party's presidential candidate. On November 3, 1992, Mr. Clinton was elected president of the country. He was 46 years old at the time. William Jefferson Clinton was inaugurated the forty-second president of the United States in Washington, D.C. on January 20, 1993.

Write a sentence summarizing this paragraph: _____

_____

_____

_____

Outline the facts in this paragraph: _____

_____

_____

_____

_____

Draw a time line of the dates:

——————————/————————/————————/————————/——————

KEEPING TRACK OF ASSIGNMENTS

Sometimes kids forget to do their assignments. These missing assignments can pile up and the student gets further and further behind.

The check sheet on the next page is designed to help you stay on top of all your assignments each week. You will need to take this sheet to each teacher every Friday. Teachers are to sign the "ALL CLEAR" if you have handed in all of your assignments for the week. They are to write down any missing assignments for you to complete over the weekend.

By completing your work weekly, you will be better prepared in class and for tests and quizzes. You will also feel better if you are up to date in your work.

Copy the check sheet and use it each Friday at school for a month. See how much it helps you.

Remember: Doing a little at a time gets the work done.

WEEKLY ASSIGNMENT CHECK SHEET

STUDENT _____

WEEK OF _____

Subject	Teacher's Signature	Assignments Handed in (yes/no)	Assignments Missing
_____	_____	_____	_____
_____	_____	_____	_____
_____	_____	_____	_____
_____	_____	_____	_____
_____	_____	_____	_____
_____	_____	_____	_____
_____	_____	_____	_____

Parent's signature _____

PLAN FOR THE MONTH

As you move into the higher grades you will find it helpful to use a calendar each month to keep track of due dates for projects and reports, dates of test, and important events you must remember. Instead of relying only on your memory you can <u>see</u> everything you need to do right in front of you. This is a great planning tool!

Here is a sample calendar:

FEBRUARY

SUNDAY	MONDAY	TUESDAY	WEDNESDAY	THURSDAY	FRIDAY	SATURDAY
1	study for science test 2	study for science test 3	science test 4	5	class trip 6	7
8	book report due 9	10	11	12	spelling test 13	14
15	No school 16	17	Jen's birthday party 18	Hand in outline for social studies project 19	spelling test 20	21
22	Rough draft of social studies project due 23	social studies project due 24	25	Dentist appointment (2:45) 26	spelling test 27	28

Buy a large calendar and keep it in your room to use for planning.

Part 5
♦♦♦
SETTING GOALS

Part of everyday life is setting goals for yourself. Becoming a better soccer player or cleaning your room over the weekend are two examples. We all have projects that must be completed. Some of these we need to do right away or very soon. Others do not have to be finished until some date far in the future. We can set personal goals for ourselves in much the same way we plan for projects. Some will be accomplished easily in a short time, but others we will need to keep working on, maybe even for the rest of our lives. The important thing is not to give up. Dream, plan, and think big to become the best that you can be.

SET A GOAL FOR YOURSELF

Is there something you would like to learn to do? Something that you could do better?

Write your goal here: _____

_____

_____

Write down the name of someone who could help you accomplish this goal:

_____

How long will you try to work on this goal?

☐ one day   ☐ three days   ☐ one week   ☐ two weeks

After that time is up, evaluate yourself.

Did you achieve your goal? _____

If you were successful, keep up the good work!

If you haven't yet achieved your goal, what could you do to be successful?

_____

_____

_____

_____

Keep trying! Don't forget to ask a helper for suggestions.

BLUE RIBBONS FOR A JOB WELL DONE

Color each of these ribbons and cut them out carefully. Give one to a parent and one to your teacher or counselor. Ask them to award a ribbon to you when you do something well or have put in a lot of effort to accomplish a goal.

MORE BLUE RIBBONS

Here are two more ribbons for you to color and cut out. Award one to your parent and one to your teacher or counselor. Award them when they have done something that is really helpful to you. Watch them smile!

IDEAS FROM OTHER KIDS

There are many kids like you who have ADHD. Here are some thoughts and comments that they have sent us to share with you. Read what they have to say.

Danielle Cherrick, Grade 6, Rockville, Maryland

"Don't just keep homework assignments in your head. Write everything down so you can look at it whenever you need to know what to do. My teacher gives us a homework sheet that helps a lot.

Don't do two things at once. Concentrate on one thing at a time so you don't overwhelm yourself."

Adam Geiger, Grade 6, Gaithersburg, Maryland

"This is how I take my notes for a report. At first, I speak my notes into a tape recorder. Later, I listen to what I said and then I type it into a computer. Then I print the information out on note cards. It is easier to do it this way than to write quickly, when you have the source in front of you."

Akiva Resnikoff, Grade 5, Berkeley, California

Akiva and his mother have found an easy way to get homework done. He does math and writing assignments with his tutor. He works on social studies homework with his mother. He reviews social studies material with his mother before each test. He takes care of all his other work independently. He is allowed one hour of TV time each night after he has finished his homework.

Francis DeRevere, Grade 8, Millbury, Massachusetts

"It seemed like a whole new world. At first, I didn't understand how it would work for me. I started taking Ritalin twice a day at school and once for homework, in junior high. After a few days, I felt a definite change, not only in my schoolwork but also in my ability to think things through. After a while it felt 'strange' to be on top of my work and have assignments and projects handed in on time. I wish we had heard about Ritalin before the 7th grade so I could have always gotten A's and B's."

Kids' Ideas *(continued)*

Meir Lax, Grade 3, Houston, Texas

Meir finds that when he has to remind himself to do something, he makes a picture in his head of the object (such as a pair of shoes that have to be put away) and "keeps" the picture there as the reminder, since talking to himself can be distracting.

Since Meir sometimes needs to fidget a little in order to listen well in class, his teachers allow him to do something quiet, such as origami, as long as he does not disturb anyone.

Meir calls his school desk a "black hole," since he can never find anything inside of it. Instead, he keeps a milk crate right next to his desk. All of his books and supplies are kept neatly lined up in the crate, where they are easy to see. Whenever he finishes his work early, Meir's teacher lets him use the extra time to organize the crate, which he discovered he enjoys doing.

Jeremy King, Grade 4, Mobile, Alabama

Jeremy plays a lot of baseball and does Tae-Kwon-Do because he is very good at both of these. This helps him to feel good about himself. He also spends lots of time with his godmother, because they have fun together. Jeremy's mom encourages him to do homework right after school while he can still focus well.

Maria Kenny, Grade 7, Washington, D.C.

Maria writes herself a daily reminder list of things she has to do, and checks it over each morning. To remember to take her noon dose of medication each day in school, Maria sets her diver's watch (which she bought in a sporting goods store). When the alarm goes off, she makes sure to leave it on until she has actually taken the medicine. Then she turns the alarm off. (If you are in a quiet classroom, this also encourages you to leave the room for the nurse's office right before the alarm goes off!)

Francesca Mancini, Grade 7, St. Paul, Minnesota

"I have two friends who also have ADHD. Neither of them takes medication. One friend tried not to eat sugar and watched her diet. She could concentrate sometimes if she was told to and she really tried very hard. The other girl could not concentrate at all. She didn't take medicine and probably should have, since nobody liked her at all because of her behavior.

"I started taking Ritalin in 1989 and it has really helped me focus on one thing at a time. It lifted the fog that had clouded my thinking, and helped me do better in reading and math."

Answers

page 22

1. attention 2. smart 3. Exercising 4. too few neurotransmitters 5. before 6. medicine
7. doctor 8. should 9. An apple 10. Lots of 11. sitting still 12. okay 13. can

page 32

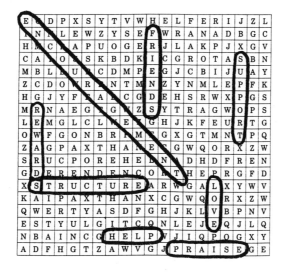

page 38

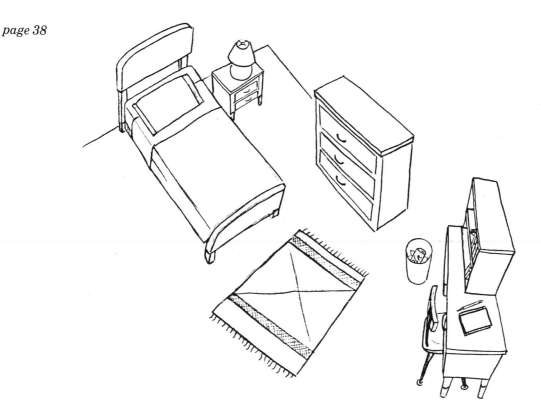

Jimmy's room all cleaned up

Answers *(continued)*

page 40

A. A vase or two faces. **B.** Both! This figure is called the Penrose Triangle. It can be drawn on paper but is impossible to build in three dimensions. **C.** A map. Usually we view the water as background for the land. In this map, the black area is the Mediterranean Sea. **D.** Both sections are the same. This is called the Muller-Lyer Illusion. This illusion is so strong that it occurs even when there is proof that the distance between arrows is the same, as with this ruler:

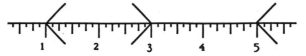

E. Close your left eye and stare with your right eye at the target. The face will disappear because light reflected from it will fall on your blind spot where nerves leave the eye to go to the brain.

page 43
A. 3, 2, 1   **B.** 2, 1, 3, 4   **C.** 1, 4, 3, 2

page 44
A. 3, 1, 4, 2   **B.** 3, 1, 2, 4   **C.** 3, 1, 4, 2

page 46

page 54
1. 63   **2.** 11   **3.** 67   **4.** 48   **5.** 24   **6.** 72   **7.** 5   **8.** 55   **9.** 269   **10.** 11,760   **11.** 93   **12.** 9¾

page 55

Last week, we went to visit my aunt and uncle, who live in Detroit, Michigan. When Aunt Jane saw me, she said in a loud voice, "You've really grown since last year!" We had fun being together. Next year, I hope we can spend more than two days in Detroit.

Glossary

Attention Deficit Hyperactivity Disorder – A condition in a person of average or above-average intelligence that includes symptoms such as short attention span, distractibility, impulsivity, and/or hyperactivity.

Brain – The major organ of the nervous system. It controls all mental and physical activities.

Brain Stem – A part of the brain that controls automatic functions such as breathing, heart rate, and blood pressure.

Cerebellum – A part of the brain that controls the movements of the muscles.

Cerebral Cortex – The outermost layer of the brain. Its networks are essential to higher thinking activities. It makes up 40% of total brain weight.

Counselor – A professional who works with children or adults to help them understand feelings and solve their problems.

Details – The small parts of something such as a story or picture. They are important to the overall meaning.

Disorder – Something that is not working the way it should.

Essential – Necessary.

Evaluate – To judge or look back and check performance.

Focusing – Paying careful attention.

Goal – The end result toward which someone works.

Hyperactive – Overactive, moving around a great deal.

Impulsive – Acting or speaking without thinking.

Inattentive – Not paying attention.

Irritable – Overly sensitive or in a bad mood.

Learning Disabilities – Difficulties in learning to read, write, or do mathematics which cause problems in school achievement.

Long-Term Assignments – Assignments that are due several days or weeks from the time first given.

Medication – Substances used to treat illnesses or to improve functioning of the body or brain. Some of the current medications used for ADHD are: Ritalin, Dexedrine, Imipramine, Cylert, and Clonidine.

Motivate – To encourage or increase a person's desire to perform a task or learn.

Neuron – A single brain cell composed of a cell body, dendrites, and an axon. Each neuron is a complex coordinator of many stimuli. Within the cell body and dendrites, there are specialized receptors that take in stimuli from other neurons.

Neurotransmitters – Chemical substances produced by brain cells that act as messengers. They cross the space (synapse) between cells and conduct a nerve message or impulse along a pathway.

Pediatrician – A medical doctor who is a specialist in the health of children and adolescents.

Prescribe – To write direction for the preparation and use of a medicine.

Proofread – Check over work for mistakes.

Reminder – Method to help remember something.

Sequencing – Putting things in their correct order.

Side Effects – Symptoms that may occur as a result of taking medicine.

Solutions – Ways to take care of a problem.

Subcortex – The area below and surrounded by the cerebral cortex. It coordinates incoming stimuli from the brain stem and other areas and sends stimuli to the cerebral cortex and other areas of the brain.

Support – A kind of help given by someone else.

Summarize – To briefly state the main idea.

Synapse – The site of contact of one neuron with another. A microscopic space (extremely small; can be seen only with a microscope) between the neurons.

Therapist – A professional who works with children and adults to solve problems, understand feelings, or change behavior. A therapist can be a counselor, social worker, psychologist, or psychiatrist.

Tutor – A person who works with children outside of class to help them learn to do better in school.

Visualize – To picture something in your mind.

Resources for Kids

◆ On ADD

Books

Galvin, Matthew. *Otto Learns About His Medicine.* Magination Press, 1988.

Gehret, Jeanne. *Eagle Eyes: A Child's View of Attention Deficit Disorder.* Verbal Images Press, 1991.

Gordon, Michael. *Jumping Johnny Get Back to Work: A Child's Guide to ADHD/Hyperactivity.* GSI Publications, 1991.

Ingersoll, Barbara D. *Distant Drums, Different Drummers.* Cape Publications, 1995.

Levine, Melvin. *Keeping A Head in School.* Educators Publishing Service, 1990.

Moss, Deborah. *Shelly, the Hyperactive Turtle.* Woodbine House, 1989.

Nadeau, Kathleen, and Dixon, Ellen. *Learning to Slow Down and Pay Attention.* New Edition. Magination Press, 1997.

Parker, Roberta, and Parker, Harvey. *Making the Grade: An Adolescent's Struggle with Attention Deficit Disorder.* Impact Publications, 1992.

Quinn, Patricia. *Adolescents and ADD: Gaining the Advantage.* Magination Press, 1995.

Quinn, Patricia, and Stern, Judith. *Putting on the Brakes: Young People's Guide to Understanding Attention Deficit Hyperactivity Disorder.* Magination Press, 1991.

Stern, Judith, and Ben-Ami, Uzi. *Many Ways to Learn: Young People's Guide to Learning Disabilities.* Magination Press, 1996.

Videotape

Goldstein, Sam, and Goldstein, Michael. "It's Just Attention Deficit Disorder." Neurology, Learning and Behavior Center, 670 East 3900 South, Suite 100, Salt Lake City, UT 84107.

◆ Feeling Good About Yourself

Books

Caffrey, Jaye. *First Star I See.* Verbal Images Press, 1997.

Cain, Barbara. *Double Dip Feelings.* Magination Press, 1991.

Espeland, Pamela, and Wallner, Rosemary. *Making the Most of Today: Daily Readings for Young People on Self-Awareness, Creativity, and Self-Esteem.* Free Spirit Publishing, 1991.

Kaufman, Gershen, and Rafael, Lev. *Stick Up for Yourself: Every Kid's Guide to Personal Power and Positive Self-Esteem.* Free Spirit Publishing, 1991.

Roberts, Barbara. *Phoebe Flowers' Adventures: That's What Kids Are For.* Advantage Books, 1998.

Schwartz, Linda. *The Month-To-Month Me (An Activity Book for Children).* The Learning Works, P.O. Box 6187, Santa Barbara, CA 93160 (1-800-235-5767).

Games

"The Stop, Relax, and Think Game" (ages 7–12). Center for Applied Psychology. Childswork/Childsplay, P.O. Box 1587, King of Prussia, PA 19406 (1-800-962-1141).

"Stress Strategies." Stress Education Center (413-484-5700).

◆ Getting Organized at Home and School

Books

Cummings, Rhoda, and Fisher, Gary. *The School Survival Guide for Kids with Learning Differences.* Free Spirit Publishing, 1991.

James, Elizabeth, and Barkin, Carol. *How to Be School Smart: Secrets of Successful Schoolwork.* Lothrop, Lee and Shepard Books, 1988.

Schwartz, Linda. *Study Skills Shortcake* (activity book, ages 9+). The Learning Works, 1979.

Computer Software

"Test Taking Made Easy" (grades 6–8). Lawrence Productions, 1800 S. 35th St., Galesburg, MI 49053 (1-800-421-4157).

"Following Directions" (grades 6–8). Lawrence Productions, 1800 S. 35th St., Galesburg, MI 49053 (1-800-421-4157).

Board Game

"Following Directions." Learning Well Co., P.O. Box 3759, New Hyde Park, NY 11040 (1-800-645-6564).

Organizational Materials

"Organizational Tools for Students in Grades 3–12" is a catalogue of useful materials for students. It contains items such as structured assignment notebooks and calendars. The catalogue can be ordered from: Success by Design, P.O. Box 957033, Hoffman Estates, IL 60195 (1-800-327-0057).